This book belongs to:

....

....

Kay Maguire · Danielle Kroll

Nature's Day

Discover the world of wonder on your doorstep

WIDE EYED EDITIONS

Contents

Introduction

Nature is everywhere—living, breathing, and growing, right under your nose. From the birds in the trees, to the mushrooms in the woods, the tadpoles in the pond and the spider in the fence at the end of your street, nature is all around you. You just need to stop a minute and look.

As the year changes from season to season, the insects, plants, and animals you see change too. In spring, the temperatures rise and the days get a little longer, buds burst into leaf, the first flowers blossom, and hibernating animals stir, knowing that finally there is food to be found. New life can be born. As the days get warmer and longer still, the sun shines and summer is here! Flowers everywhere bloom, fruits ripen, and birds and animals fill their days feeding their young. The days go by and the weather starts to change again. Days are cooler and shorter, and with less light from the sun, the last flowers fade and turn to seed. Berries appear, and animals and birds feast on the fall harvest, preparing for the cold weather and the lack of food ahead. Then, finally, the weather turns to ice, plants start to die, and the lean days of winter arrive. All is still as the plants and the animals hide from the cold, dark days—until suddenly, the ice melts, the sun shines, and the flowers begin to bloom. A whole year has passed and it's spring again!

The year has come full circle, and each beautiful season will keep on coming, again and again, with its own unique and wonderful things to see. This book will help you find those things and discover the world of wonder that is on your doorstep.

Welcome to SPRING

After a long, cold winter, nature is finally stirring! Every day, it gets warmer and the days get a little brighter and longer. Buds open, shoots sprout, and early flowers burst into bloom. As the soil gets warmer, spring bulbs push up through the ground and newly-sown seeds germinate and begin to grow.

Spring is a season of new beginnings. Lambs are born and skip happily in the fields, rabbits leave their burrows, and birds arrive and start to build nests, singing as they work. The world is waking up! So stop for a moment and look around you.

The World Awakes

The garden is a wonderful place in spring, as everything, at last, begins to grow and flower. On warmer days, we can go outside and explore: smell the sweet scent of the shrubs and trees in bloom; peer under stones and look for centipedes, worms, and wood lice; and watch the first bees buzz around the flowers. When you wake up early in the morning, lie still and close your eyes so you can hear the birds. The garden can be a noisy place in spring!

The dawn chorus is loudest in spring, as many birds try to attract a mate by singing.

Can you hear the birds singing, greeting the dawn? Day after day, they repeat this song, which is called the dawn chorus.

Tweet tweet! Tweet tweet!

Birds sing at dawn to claim their territories and to let other birds know where they are.

The chorus gets louder and louder as more birds add their chirps, whistles, and warbles to the song.

Birds mate in spring, when it is warm and there is lots of food around for their chicks.

Tweet tweet! Tweet tweet!

The same birds start the chorus every day. Robins, blackbirds, and song sparrows are some of the first to sing.

The low light at dawn makes it a bad time for birds to forage for food, but a good time to make a lot of noise without getting caught by predators!

Salad Days

Spring is the busiest time in the vegetable patch, with seeds being sown and the first crops ready to harvest. The soil is warmer now, the perfect temperature for seeds to start sending out shoots. As the land wakes up, weeds also start to appear and need to be cleared away. The soil is raked and watered, ready for the new seeds to be sown.

The slender green spikes of asparagus poke up through the soil and stretch, waiting to be cut and eaten with a crunch.

Potatoes are planted now, buried deep in the earth with their little knobbly shoots ready to start growing.

Give the long pink stalks of rhubarb a tug and cut off the leaves, and they are ready to go in a yummy pie or crumble.

It's seed-sowing time! Make a hole or draw a line with your finger and sprinkle them in. Then give them a drink and wait for new green shoots to appear.

Weeds grow quickly and produce lots of seeds very fast. Pull them out before they cover the crops and stop them from growing. Look out for worms wiggling through the soil!

Bees are abuzz around the white flowers of strawberries, drinking their nectar and pollinating as they go. Watch the yellow centers of each flower. Soon the petals will fall and what remains will swell and redden into plump, juicy strawberries.

The first fresh green lettuce leaves will be ready to be picked soon and eaten in an early spring salad.

Lettuce

Slugs and snails love spring—there are plenty of fresh, young leaves for them to eat. Follow their slimy, glistening trails or look for holes in leaves; they won't be far away!

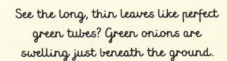

Pull the leafy tuft of a radish and find the marbles of red and white below.

See the long, thin leaves like perfect green tubes? Green onions are swelling just beneath the ground.

Below fine, feathery leaves, bright orange carrots are reaching down through the soil.

Some tree flowers are tiny, almost unseen in yellow and green but catkins are easy to spot, hanging in golden clusters from bare brown branches.

Look for splashes of color among the brown leaves on the woodland floor. Bright bluebells, white anemones, and purple violets are coming into flower.

Birds are hard at work collecting twigs, moss, and leaves for their nests. When they are done, they will sit and wait for their eggs to hatch.

The new leaves of ferns slowly unfurl in a spiral of soft green growth.

Songs of Spring

The woods are a noisy place in spring! Birds are arriving from colder countries far away, making friends and building nests ready for egg laying and the arrival of their newly-hatched chicks. Trees are waking up after their long winter sleep, while woodland flowers make the most of the spring sunshine still streaming through the almost-bare trees, and burst into bloom.

The woods are full of sound—woodpeckers are pecking at trees, cuckoos are calling, and tree creepers are flitting from trunk to trunk.

At last! The neat, tight buds burst into leaf, opening their bright new growth to the light and casting shadows on the ground.

Stop and smell the air. Wild garlic is filling the woods with its bitter, garlicky scent.

Look carefully on the woodland floor. Popping up through the leaves are tiny tree seedlings: young trees that are growing where seeds fell months before.

15

New Life

With winter over and the weather getting warmer, the farmer opens the barn doors wide and lets the animals out into the fields again. Cows, pigs, goats, and sheep all scamper outside, delighted to be in the spring sunshine.

As the days get longer and the sun rises earlier, the cockerel celebrates the start of the day with a cheery "Cock-a-doodle-doo!" each morning at dawn, while the hens are busy laying eggs again after their winter's rest. But spring can be a tiring time for the farmer with lots of animals being born—often in the middle of the night.

Calves can stand by themselves within just a few minutes of being born, but they still need to be taken care of by their mothers until they are strong enough to walk and run well.

Most piglets are born in the spring, staying close to their mothers until they are ready to go out into the fields. There may be as many as twelve little piglets in every litter.

After a winter indoors, the cows are finally let out to pasture. See them run and skip in the sunshine, off to find the best grass to eat.

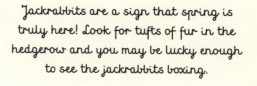

Jackrabbits are a sign that spring is truly here! Look for tufts of fur in the hedgerow and you may be lucky enough to see the jackrabbits boxing.

17

Plowing the Fields

The land comes alive in spring with trees and hedgerows finally turning a fresh, bright green. Autumn-sown crops start to sprout and grow, and in empty fields, the farmer is out in his tractor with his plow on the back, getting ready to sow new crops. Later in the season, fields flash with gold as rapeseed bursts into flower. As the hedgerows fill with leaves and blossoms, birds, bees, mice, and shrews flutter and scuttle from field to field.

The bright yellow fields dotting the countryside are planted with rapeseed, a plant in the same family as cabbages. Rapeseed produces oil that we use for cooking.

In between fields, the hedgerows are a jumble of trees, shrubs, and brambles. Early in spring, the white flowers of the downy hawthorn are among the first to appear.

In spring, the farmer is busy on his tractor, plowing the fields and drilling the soil to ready it for seeds.

Look at the sky. Can you spot any shapes as the clouds drift by?

In spring, the fields are turning from brown to green as crops of wheat, corn, and maize start pushing up through the soil.

How loud the birds are squawking behind the tractor as the plow turns the soil! They are following it closely, looking for worms or seeds to eat.

Just before the end of spring, hawthorn bursts into flower. It is often called mayflower after the month that it blooms. The bees love its white flowers.

Perfect Weather for Ducks

The pond is full of life in spring. Newts and water snails emerge from a winter spent burrowed down in the sludge at the bottom, frog spawn laid by returning frogs in late winter sits in large jelly clumps in the water, and toad spawn hangs from water plants in chains.

Toads are very fussy about where they lay their eggs and often travel all the way back to the pond where they were born just to mate, so if you see a toad crossing the road, give it a hand because that's where it's going! Frog spawn begins to change in spring, as their eggs grow tails and legs, until finally they become tiny froglets.

Look closely at the swans: nestled among their feathers are little cygnets, hitching a ride on Mom's or Dad's back.

Along the water's edge, the golden flowers of marsh marigolds and strange skunk cabbage shelter the first frogs.

Fluffy ducklings hatch in spring and take to the water, following their mother wherever she goes. Can you hear her quacking at them to stay close?

The sky-blue flowers of water forget-me-nots are the perfect hiding place for small amphibians like newts.

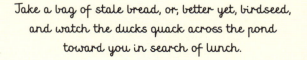

Take a bag of stale bread, or, better yet, birdseed, and watch the ducks quack across the pond toward you in search of lunch.

Blossoming Trees

Orchards are beautiful in spring, with buttercups and daisies in the grass and the trees a mass of pink and white blossoms. Bees and butterflies dart from flower to flower, drinking nectar and pollinating the blossoms so that later in the year they will grow into fruit like apples, cherries, pears, and plums. As a breeze blows, blossoms fall from the trees and cover the ground like snow.

Caterpillars are eating a lot, munching on leaves and quickly getting bigger, ready for the day they spin themselves a cocoon and then become a beautiful butterfly or moth.

Nettles are covered in tiny stinging hairs. They make the perfect place for butterflies to lay their eggs, keeping the caterpillars safe from being eaten.

Flowers growing in among the trees open one by one. They are full of nectar for the bees, who collect it to make their sweet and sticky honey.

Bees are always a sign that spring has arrived. The queen bee, the mother of all the bees in a hive, is the first to be seen.

Fruit trees are smothered in pink and white blossoms, which fall to the ground like confetti.

Large dock leaves often grow in clumps near stinging nettles. If you get stung, rub on a leaf and it will ease the pain.

If you're very still, you might see rabbits sitting in the grass, twitching their noses. If they hear you coming, they'll hop off!

Color takes the place of gray as cherry and magnolia trees burst into leaf and flower.

On brighter days, people come outside to wash and spring-clean their cars.

Sunny daffodil trumpets burst into bloom, brightening the day.

Look out for squirrels scurrying from tree to tree in search of food, hungry after the long, lean winter.

Birds are settling down in their nests, ready to lay eggs and meet their new chicks.

Unlike lots of birds, pigeons mate for life. Can you hear the couples cooing to each other?

Birds love drinking from puddles, making the most of any rainfall to quench their thirst.

Spring Clean

The street becomes a different place in spring. Trees and plants turn green and start to flower, while bulbs push their way through the soil and break into bloom. Squirrels and birds appear, braving the day in search of food and drink, and people leave their winter coats indoors, happy to be enjoying life outside again. Lawns are mown, cars washed, and windows cleaned.

Welcome to SUMMER

The days are long, the weather is warm, and the sun shines brightly in the sky. Color is everywhere as flowers burst into bloom and crops swell and ripen. Farmers are busy—out on their tractors collecting hay and shearing sheep, cutting their long, shaggy coats for wool. Gardens and vegetable patches are like jungles: full of growth. Birds sing, butterflies flutter, and bees fill the air with their sleepy hum. Picnic blankets are laid with food as grass blows gently in the breeze, and children are busy making daisy chains while the sun beats down from the sky. Grab a hat and get outside!

Garden Blooms

The summer garden is full of color and life. The sun shines warmly and brightly in the sky, and the air is filled with the fragrance of flowers.

Plants bloom in every shade, from red and pink to orange, yellow, and blue, while butterflies and bees dart from flower to flower, drinking their sugary liquid called nectar. Close your eyes and listen to the buzz of bees, the singsong twitter of birds, and the hum of a distant lawn mower.

Bright butterflies flit between the blooms, using their long tongues, called a proboscis, to sip at nectar.

The golden heads of sunflowers follow the sun as it moves across the sky. See the bees clustering in their dusky centers, drinking the nectar.

Did you know blackbirds jump up and down on grass to get worms to pop up? When they spot them, they pull them out with their beaks to eat.

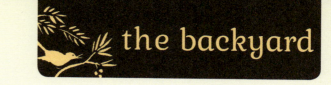

The garden is a mass of gorgeous colors and scents in summer as flowers, shrubs, and climbers all burst into bloom.

Not all striped black-and-yellow insects are wasps and bees—hoverflies look just like them but have no sting. Watch them dart silently among the flowers.

If you spot mounds of soil, like tiny volcanoes in the lawn, sit and watch for little mining bees buzzing in and out. Beneath the ground are their nests, full of busy bees.

The hum of a lawn mower is one of the sounds of the summer; grass grows fast and needs mowing once a week to keep it neat.

Plants use color and scent to attract bees and butterflies. One of the bees' favorite flowers is lavender, and they love to buzz around its sweet-smelling, nectar-full blooms.

Ruby ladybugs are a gardener's best friends—they love plant-munching aphids and can eat more than fifty in just one day!

Ripe for Picking

It's a happy, busy time on the vegetable patch as crops everywhere ripen in the warm sunshine and are soon ready to pick and eat.

Frosts have passed, warm fleeces and protective cloches can be put away, and watering and weeding need to be done—sometimes every day to make sure there are plenty of fruits and vegetables for all. Everything is growing: zucchinis swell, beans and peas fill their pods, and juicy red strawberries and tomatoes are delicious eaten straight from the plant.

Zucchinis are swelling and getting ready to be eaten. Did you know you can eat their flowers too?

After the pretty red flowers have faded, long, thin, green beans appear. Keep picking and more beans will come!

The long green bunches of tomatoes are called trusses. Leave the fruits to ripen to a deep red and then pop one in your mouth!

Poke around in the soil with your fingers and you should feel the firm tops of carrots beneath their feathery leaves. Give them a gentle pull and see what you get.

Strawberries are one of the best things about summer! Warmed by the sun, they grow red, sweet, and juicy.

Pick the crisp green leaves of lettuce just before you want to eat them, pulling them gently with your finger and thumb.

Their flowers tell you that potatoes are growing in the soil. When the flowers die away, the potatoes are ready.

Juicy red currants, blueberries, and raspberries hang like jewels and are ready to pick when they are plump and firm.

Keep an eye out for white butterflies fluttering around the cabbage patch. Their hungry black-and-yellow caterpillars will be eating holes in the leaves somewhere nearby.

Slugs and snails hide in dark, damp places in summer, coming out at night and early in the morning to munch on young leaves and plants.

Pull out any weeds, which take valuable food and water from your crops, and add them to the compost heap.

You can see when peas are plump in their pods and ready to be picked. Run your thumb along the pod and pop out the peas—straight into your mouth to eat!

Aphids are tiny black or green flies that munch plants. Happily, the wonderful ladybug eats the aphids.

Summer is a thirsty time for plants, and they need lots of water in the hot, dry weather. Keep watering seeds sown at the end of the summer, and you will have delicious vegetables early in spring next year.

Birds hop from branch to branch calling to each other and filling the woods with their chirping, tweeting song.

Stand still and listen to the soft rustle of wind in the leaves as a breeze blows through the woods and the treetops sway back and forth.

Sweet-smelling honeysuckle twines its way through the branches, reaching for the light.

You might spot pink or yellow bumps and lumps on leaves. An insect has been eating them, and the tree has made the bumps, or galls, to protect itself.

The bramble's thorny branches are covered in flowers, which will become black juicy fruit in a few weeks' time.

If you crunch on a pinecone underfoot, pick it up and look at it. Has a squirrel or a mouse taken a bite?

Be careful on the woodland path! Trails of ants are on the march, but where are they going and where have they been?

Shiny black beetles, wood lice, and centipedes live in nooks and crannies under logs and in piles of leaves. Carefully lift some up and see what you can find.

Woodland Walks

The woods are a quieter, more peaceful place in summer. Trees are in full leaf, casting shadows on the woodland floor, while the gentle whistle of birds lilts through the cool shade. See the bright shafts of sunlight through the leaves, listen to the birdsong and the rustle of wind in the trees, smell the warm, damp earth, and look quietly for animals on the move.

If you're in the woods as the sun sets, look up—bats are swooping for insects while owls silently listen for the scuttle of their prey.

Very soon the eggs in the nests up above will crack open, and hungry, chirping baby birds will pop out.

Deer quietly graze on leaves and grass in the cool canopy of the trees. Don't make a sound or they'll run away.

Almost hidden on the woodland floor are burrows: holes in the ground that are doorways to the homes of rabbits, badgers, or foxes.

The bright pink flowers of the red campion take the place of bluebells, carpeting the woodland floor.

Look out for small brown pellets on the ground that could be the droppings of foxes, rabbits, or deer, but don't touch it with your hands—poke it with a stick instead!

Long, Hot Days

Farm animals love to spend the long summer days outside in the warm, bright sunshine. The yard is busy with scampering chickens and geese fighting over the best seeds to eat, and the fields are dotted with grazing cows, flocks of sheep, and hungry, foraging pigs. With plenty of grass to eat and water from the farmer, they have everything they need. The farmer rises early in the morning, ready to start the day, and works, busy with the animals, until the sun finally sets in the sky.

At the end of the day, the farmer leads the cows—udders heavy with milk—out of the fields and into the shed for milking.

All day long, the hens and the geese in the farmyard peck at the ground looking for seeds, grain, insects, and worms to eat.

Barn owls hunt for mice, shrews, and voles at night. Did you know that they screech rather than hoot?

Grass grows quickly in summer. Nestled among the blades are the round, flat leaves of clover, a favorite flower of bees.

The days are long on the farm in summer, with busy early mornings and slow afternoons, stretching into warm, bright evenings, until the sun finally sets.

The stumpy spikes of plantain begin to flower in the meadow, their seeds held in a pretty frill around the spike.

Pigs, living outdoors for the summer, hunt out the shade on the brightest days to stop themselves getting burned by the sun.

Fluttering along the hedgerows are beautiful blue butterflies, their wings sparkling like jewels in the sunshine.

When the crops are cut, the straw that is left behind is laid out to dry in the sun and become hay. Bundled into bales, it is used as winter food for the animals when there is no fresh grass to eat.

A kestrel—always hungry—is ready to dive and pounce on an unsuspecting mouse.

The sound of chitter-chatter up above is the skylark climbing and singing as it flies.

Tiny harvest mice scuttle through the field, climbing up stalks of grass and grains to get to the seeds.

The grasshopper sings its clicking, chirping song by rubbing its back legs together before leaping off across the field.

Hedgerows are full of dense leaves now, becoming tunnels that help animals and insects scuttle from field to field unseen.

Wildflowers bloom around the edge of the field—scarlet poppies, bright blue cornflowers, and giant oxeye daisies.

Making Hay in the Sunshine

The warm summer sun helps the farmer's crops to ripen well in the field. Wheat, corn, barley, and oats turn golden and brown, ready to be cut and harvested at the end of the summer. When they are ripe, the farmer gets into his tractor and drives, up and down, back and forth across the fields, cutting the crops. Birds watch from up above, butterflies float lazily around the meadow edge, and insects, mice, and foxes hide in the cool of the hedgerow.

Splashing Around

The pond is a magical place in summer. Water plants are in full leaf and flower and become helpful hiding places for newly emerging froglets, toadlets, and baby newts. The water is busy with insects crisscrossing its surface, while underneath, the roots of floating plants bury themselves deep in the mud to take hold, as snails, water beetles, small fish, and dragonfly larvae flit by. On warm mornings, these larvae leave the water, climb high onto a plant to dry their new wings in the sun, and then zoom off. If you look closely, you just might find the larval cases they have left behind.

As the day turns to night, foraging bats skim above the surface of the pond looking for a mid-flight feast of tasty midges and flies.

Pond skaters whiz across the surface of the water, while just below, water boatmen paddle their long legs gracefully around the pond.

Down below, young newts use their long tails to help them swim swiftly through the water, ready to leave the pond at the end of the summer.

Tiny new froglets and toadlets emerge from the water and take their first hops and steps, looking for worms and slugs to eat.

If you're quiet—and very lucky—you might spot a cold-blooded grass snake basking in the morning sunshine, warming itself before sliding off in search of food.

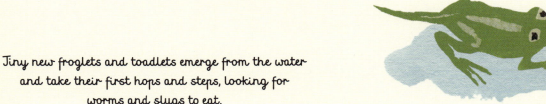

On cooler, less sunny days, frogs and toads sing their warbly croak to attract a mate.

The round, flat leaves and pretty flowers of the water lily float on the water, while close by the iris's sword-like leaves point to the sky.

On still summer days, colorful dragonflies zoom and dart in zigzags across the pond.

A long-legged heron stands at the water's edge, silently waiting to grab a fish with its dagger-shaped beak.

Clumps of fuzzy brown bulrushes stand tall around the banks of the pond, the perfect place for newts and frogs to take shelter in .

Ducks and moorhens use their webbed feet to walk quickly through the mud and then hop into the water for a cooling swim.

Fruit-Laden Boughs

The orchard is heavenly in summer. As the last blossom falls from the trees, fruits start to swell and grow. Their skins turn from green to yellow, orange, and red, and the smell of their sweet perfume begins to fill the air. Wasps and bees visit, drawn by the smell, and birds wait patiently, ready to peck at the ripening fruit. Heavy branches start to droop, rabbits hop through the long grass, and the first ripe fruits litter the ground.

The gentle, drowsy buzz of bees and wasps fills the air; the sound made by their tiny wings beating together as they fly.

Apples on the sunniest side of the tree ripen first, their red, yellow, and green skins darkening. Pick the pears crisp and early, and let them sweeten and soften at home.

Rabbits are out, their noses twitching, in broad daylight on warm days. If you miss them, their round brown droppings are a sure sign they're nearby.

The fragrant honey smell of ripe fruit brings buzzing wasps and bees to the orchard, hoping to find something sugary to eat.

Tangy cherries hang like earrings in ruby-red bunches on the tree. Pick them quickly, before the birds eat them all!

Underneath hills of fresh, damp soil, a mole burrows and tunnels his way through the ground. Soil is piled up behind him; if you're very lucky, you might see it moving as he digs.

When plums start to fall from the tree, they are ripe for picking—firm and juicy with a rich, fragrant smell.

Soft, fuzzy peaches; smooth, round nectarines; and musky orange apricots all ripen and sweeten in the warmth of the sun.

Foxes trot from one trash can to the next, rummaging for scraps to eat.

Cracks in the sidewalk and walls are home to the purple blooming branches of buddleia and the tall pink flower spikes of fireweed.

As the sky turns dark and streetlights click on, look up for the silhouettes of fluttering moths drawn by their bright glow.

Children bike up and down, enjoying the sunshine and filling the street with the sounds of their laughter.

Baskets hanging from lampposts and doorways bring a flash of color up high.

As you walk down the street, the trees are full of leaves and summer blooms, filling the sky above your head with flowers.

Street Life

In summer, the street is full of noise, bustle, and life. Children run and bike, people are out in their yards and gardens, and the sidewalks are full as people leave their cars behind.

Trees are a mass of cool leaves and flowers, and gardens, window boxes, and baskets are full of color. Flowers buzz with butterflies and bees, and as day becomes night, moths hover around street lamps and foxes sniff out food for their young.

Garden and roadside hedges burst into bloom; breathe in the sweet, heavy scent of their creamy-white flowers.

Welcome to
FALL

Fall is a blaze of color as the leaves change on the trees and the sun hangs low in the sky. As the weeks go by, the days get shorter and there's a chill in the air when the sun disappears at the end of the day. Leaves pile up as trees become bare and birds fly south as the first icy frosts arrive. Early fall mists float across the fields while the farmer plows the land and the smoky smell of bonfires fills the air. It's time to dig out your scarf and gloves and run and swish through the rustling leaves. Crouch down low to explore and look up high, through the disrobed branches of the trees.

Flying South to the Sun

The garden is quiet in fall as birds leave, flying to warm places to escape the cold. Insects, butterflies, and small animals look for shelter against the harsh weather and the leaves on the trees turn orange, yellow, and red before falling to reveal new shapes and silhouettes. Most flowers fade, but a few late bloomers bring a flash of welcome color. Bright berries appear on bushes, and trees and seedheads stand tall, adding a warm shade of brown.

Fading rose flowers are replaced with bright scarlet hips, too large for smaller birds to eat but a delicious snack for blackbirds and other larger birds.

Noisy magpies chatter in the trees, hopping from branch to branch, waiting for something to catch their eye.

As the golden petals of the sunflower turn brown and fall to the ground, the seeds at their center ripen to a dark brown, ready to be plucked out and eaten by hungry birds.

The elder is laden with bunches of purple-black berries, which are easily spotted by passing birds and a juicy autumn treat for mice and squirrels.

Lots of plants die down, sleeping beneath the ground until the spring. The seedheads they leave behind are full of tasty seeds for the birds and mice and make a cozy home for ladybugs.

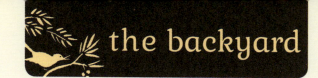

As the nights get colder, migrating butterflies head off in search of the sun, while those left behind prepare to hibernate through the winter.

Birds are on the move, flocking together, ready to fly south, until suddenly they take to the sky and are gone.

Cup-shaped flowers of the fall crocus push up through the grass beneath trees, lending it a purple glow.

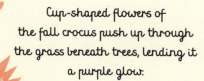

Hunt for spiderwebs strung between branches first thing in the morning. Are they glistening with the diamond drops of dew or white with frost?

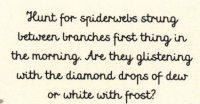

The round pom-pom heads of dahlias and chrysanthemums flower all through the fall in the warm shades of red, purple, yellow, and pink.

Crouch down on the lawn and look for worm casts: small heaps of silky brown soil that a worm has left behind.

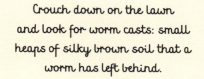

Grasses are in full flower in fall with fluffy yellow and red tufts towering on tall stems.

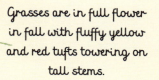

Late Bloomers

The first frosts of fall signal the end of the harvest for lots of crops. Tomatoes are collected, chilies picked and dried, and the last potatoes pulled from the ground. Pumpkins are left to swell to a deep orange for Halloween, and the bare earth is dug over and left to the hard winter frosts.

Glossy purple-black eggplants hang on their prickly stalks. Pick them quickly before they turn dull and bitter.

Harvest plump, bobbly raspberries by giving them a gentle pull when they are a bright, ripe pink.

Dig around the last potatoes, then rummage with your hands and lift them, round and muddy, from the soil.

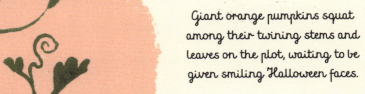

Giant orange pumpkins squat among their twining stems and leaves on the plot, waiting to be given smiling Halloween faces.

Fiery chilies and sweet peppers shine in the late-fall sun, slowly turning from green to red.

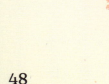

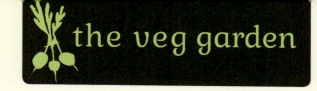

Collect the seeds of your favorite crops—tomatoes, beans, and pumpkins—dry them out and save them for sowing again next year.

Once their long leaves turn yellow, lift onions from the soil and hang them up to dry in the sun.

When the crops are done, clear them away and spread dark, crumbly compost across the bare earth, food for next year's plants.

Put the extra carrots and potatoes in large brown sacks and tuck them away in the shed—stored and ready to eat when you need them over winter.

ROOTS

Cloches, like tiny greenhouses, shelter fragile young plants, protecting them from the freezing frost.

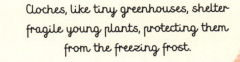

Take a spade and dig, dig, dig through the soil, turning it over, ready for the sowing of new crops next spring.

Falling Leaves

It's a magical time in the woods! The trees are full of color as the leaves turn from green to the fiery shades of fall. As they fall to the ground or blow away on the wind, they leave the bare statues of the trees behind.

The leafy carpet on the woodland floor crunches as you walk, and squirrels scurry along branches in search of nuts for their winter store. . . . Fingers crossed they remember where they hide them!

As the weather gets damper, mushrooms and toadstools in yellow, brown, and even red appear overnight, clustered around the base of trees and nestled among the fallen leaves.

Scaly pinecones, with their seeds tucked safely inside, and spiky green pine needles litter the woodland floor, blown by the wind or dropped by branches.

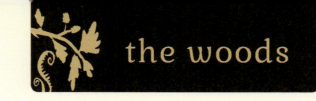

Catch and collect a leaf in
every color as they fall from up
above—green, red, yellow, orange,
purple, and brown.

As the weather gets colder, tiny
mice gather together in cozy nests,
sleeping in groups to keep warm.

Acorns still in their cups,
dark, spiky beechnuts and glossy
chestnuts drop to the ground.
Will they start to grow into trees
next spring?

As you kick through the leaves, look out
for fragile leaf skeletons. The softer parts
of the leaf are gone, leaving only the
veins—the skeleton of the leaf.

Leaves in every shape and
color carpet the ground, heaped in deep piles
and blown by the wind. Hear them rustle and
crunch as you wade through them.

Harvest Festival

The growing season is almost at an end, and after all the sowing and planting, growing and watering, the harvest is ready! Crisp, ripe vegetables and sweet, juicy fruits are picked and washed, and the very best are chosen for the county fair. The smell of ripe fruit fills the air as tables are laid with baskets, boxes, and plates full of produce, colorful jars of pickles and jams, and freshly baked cakes, cookies, and bread: a celebration of the delicious food grown this year!

Every fall across the country, farmers' markets, harvest festivals, and county fairs celebrate the harvest.

Colorful triangles of festive bunting are strung from end to end, straw bales line the floor, and tables groan under the weight of the harvest.

FARMER'S MARKET

Crisp apples for eating and cooking are picked and stored in boxes and barrels ready for the winter.

Tomatoes

Wash and chop, bubble and boil to make pickles and jams. Fill jars with the taste of summer, and enjoy them through the seasons to come!

Which is the sweetest: raspberry, the crunchiest carrot, the longest bean, the tangiest tomato? Who will win the best in show?

Bedding Down for Winter

As the weather and days draw in, the farmer is out in the fields, making the most of the shortening daylight hours. The tractor plows the earth, mud flying from its wheels, as it gets the ground ready for new crops of wheat. The hedgerows give one last burst of color as they fill with berries before losing their leaves, and the mice, shrews, and squirrels seek out thick, tussocky grasses to settle down into for the winter.

Butterflies save energy by closing their wings and hibernating in tree hollows, stone walls, and farm buildings, safely hidden from the worst of the weather.

The hedgerow is laden with bright, juicy berries—delicious pickings for the birds and a valuable source of vitamins and energy when the ground is too frozen to hunt for worms.

As the sun rises above the fields, a smoky mist creeps in through the trees and hedges until it hangs still, just above the ground.

The farmer plows the fields on the tractor; digging the soil, turning it over, and leaving behind long neat rows of fresh dark earth ready for seeds.

As food becomes scarce, mice get ready to spend the colder days in hibernation, settling down in nests of leaves, grass, and twigs to survive the winter.

55

Still Waters

Leaves land on the surface of the pond, floating until they slowly sink into the water below. The surface of the water is still as the insects that were busy all summer fly off in search of safe spots to hibernate. Frogs and newts swim to the silty bottom before the water freezes and toads crawl off to a safe, dry place to hide from the cold. Pond plants start to die back for the winter and the once-clear water turns to an inky black.

Ducks, geese, and swans gather in flocks ready to fly to warmer wetlands for the winter.

As temperatures drop, frogs swim to the bottom of the pond to burrow into the mud and muck and sleep, while toads scurry off to find their new winter homes.

Pond flowers fade and seedheads begin to form—food for visiting birds and the perfect winter hiding place for toads.

The surface of the pond is littered with the fallen leaves from nearby trees. Pond plants start to turn brown and die down for winter.

Before it gets too cold, the last insect larvae emerge and leave the pond, heading off in search of food and shelter.

Frogs and toads hunt for slugs, spiders, and insects, fattening themselves up before winter. They flick out their sticky tongues to catch their prey.

Fallen Fruits

The air is filled with the scent of overripe fruit and the buzz of greedy wasps. High autumn winds blow the last apples, pears, and plums to the ground with a thud, and the orchard floor becomes scattered with fruit. Birds nibble, wasps hum, and small animals, looking for food to see them through the winter, make a feast of fallen fruit before the frosts strike.

Blackbirds and thrushes peck at the windfall fruit scattered on the ground—it gives them lots of energy for the winter.

Leaves flutter and fall to the floor, revealing the bare, twisted stems and outline of the trees.

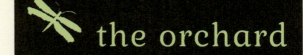

Mushrooms and toadstools push their white, yellow, and golden-brown heads through the grass in clumps, but don't pick them—they're not for eating.

Fallen branches and dead, decaying wood become home to the many beautiful beetles that depend on the orchard for food.

Foraging wasps buzz loudly around the fruit on the ground. They love the extra-sugary sweetness of the rotting flesh.

Shiny brown hazelnuts and wrinkly walnuts start to fall from their trees, ripe and ready for harvest inside their soft green cases.

Helicopter seeds flutter, spin, and twirl to the ground while bunches of ash seeds dangle, ready to drop.

A honking flock of geese flies by in a V shape, heading somewhere warm to spend the winter.

Spiky green balls with shiny conkers inside drop to the ground and split open.

Play a game of conkers! Hang them on strings and bash, bang, and smash them until they break.

Leaves pile up in drifts on the sidewalk, twirling in a whirl as the wind catches them.

Ivy clings to walls and fences with its tiny, sticky roots and is abuzz with late bees and butterflies flocking to its yellow flowers.

As light fades, the grinning faces of Halloween jack-o'-lanterns glow in windows and doorways.

Windswept Streets

The street is changing again. Fall colors are everywhere as summer flowers turn to seed, and the leaves in the trees go from green to red, yellow, orange, and brown. Bright berries and hips appear, and nuts and seeds crunch on the sidewalk as you walk. Look up through bare branches at the geese calling as they fly by. Chase a flurry of leaves as the wind whirls them down the street. Carve a spooky pumpkin for Halloween and light the candle as the sun sets.

Welcome to **WINTER**

The days are short and the long, freezing nights let you know that winter is definitely here. The world has turned from green to gray, and there is little sign of life in the garden or in the fields, as both plants and animals hide from the cold. Fires are lit, while outside, frost paints pictures on the ground and icicles hang from the bare branches of the trees.

A sudden flurry of snow turns everything white as each swirling flake covers the land in its wintry blanket. Wrap yourself up against the cold and go out into the frost and snow. Build a snowman, chase footprints, hunt for icicles, chuck a snowball, and let a snowflake melt on your tongue.

Winter Wonderland

All is still in the winter garden. Each morning, the grass is covered with a crisp white frost, and bushes and trees, empty of their leaves, have become twiggy black skeletons. Bare brown earth is dotted with the few plants that keep their leaves over the winter, while deep underground, other plants are waiting for the spring. Winter birds visit to search for food, but the garden robin is watching, ready to chase them away.

Hang a birdhouse on a tree or wall to be ready for the spring, and little blue tits and wrens may use it for a winter snooze.

As water starts to freeze, birds can struggle to find something to drink. Top up your birdbath every day and float an apple in the water to stop it freezing completely.

A flash of red is a plump robin, fluffed up against the cold, looking for food. If you go out in the garden, he will follow you.

The spiky stems of heathers are a fuzz of pink, white, and purple as they flower through the cold and snow.

Look for clusters of ladybugs in the corner of the shed, on the fence, and huddled together on plants and seedheads.

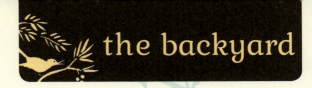

Birds need lots of energy to get through the winter. Hang up fat balls and sprinkle the bird feeder with seeds, cheese, fruit, and bread to help them survive.

Some plants hold on to their leaves in winter. These evergreen bushes and trees become the shape and color of the garden.

Spiderwebs hang on the fence and among branches, each delicate strand thick with sparkling frost.

The seedheads that flowers have left behind—feathery, spiky, and fluffy— glisten with their sprinkling of frost.

The bare branches of forsythia are covered in golden-yellow flowers, which bloom brightly long before the leaves appear.

Before it melts, go out and run on the frosty lawn and turn to look at the crunching footprints you leave behind.

Wrap up warm, lie down in the freshly fallen snow, and make snow angels, moving your arms and legs up and down, up and down!

Roots and Shoots

Winter is a time of roots and leaves at the vegetable patch. Sweeter and tastier once they have been "kissed" by the frost, wait until the weather freezes to harvest parsnips, leeks, rutabagas, and cabbages. Delicious in warming soups and stews, they are the perfect comfort food on a cold winter day! Dig and prepare the ground to ready it for the new growth in spring and wait—dreaming of the new crops to come. . . .

Tents of soft white fleece cover young crops, protecting them against the biting cold and keeping them warm until the spring.

The long pale roots of parsnips lie just below the surface, growing sweeter with every frost.

Leeks line up in straight rows of green, waiting to be pulled from the earth whenever you need them.

Half in, half out, purple-green rutabagas sit in the soil. Pull their leafy tops, and the smooth, round globes will be revealed.

Cabbages in neat green balls lie next to rows of white knobbly cauliflowers, nestled in their leafy beds.

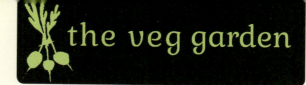

Huddled among the leaves, Brussels sprouts, like tiny cabbages, appear on their long stems—ready for Christmas dinner!

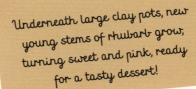

Underneath large clay pots, new young stems of rhubarb grow, turning sweet and pink, ready for a tasty dessert!

Wood is piled high for a bonfire, but wait! Check for hibernating creatures sleeping among the branches first.

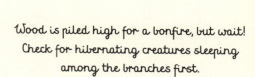

Birds hop hopefully across the hard brown earth, wishing a worm would pop up for them to eat.

On clear days, gardeners dig the earth with a spade, lifting and turning the soil, getting it ready for planting and sowing in the spring.

Crisp, glittering snow on the roof of the shed and the ground below catches the last of the day's sun.

67

Bare Branches

As you walk through the woods, the only sound is your feet on the frosty ground. The trees are bare of leaves, and the gray sky is now visible through their tangle of branches. A bird flits through the treetops, while down on the ground, the leaf litter and soil start to crisp as the temperature turns to freezing. There is little sign of life, but look carefully and you will see a footprint here, a dropping there: proof that animals stir on brighter days.

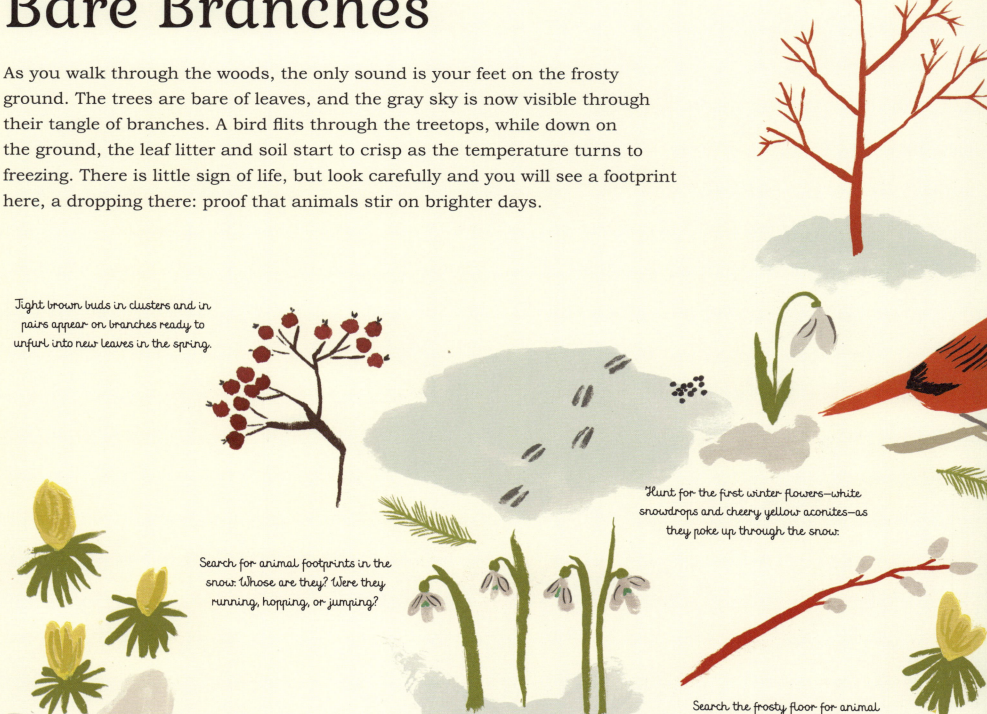

Tight brown buds in clusters and in pairs appear on branches ready to unfurl into new leaves in the spring.

Hunt for the first winter flowers—white snowdrops and cheery yellow aconites—as they poke up through the snow.

Search for animal footprints in the snow. Whose are they? Were they running, hopping, or jumping?

Search the frosty floor for animal droppings, brown against the white ground. A rabbit's are small and round, a deer's pointy and smooth.

The tap, tap, tap of a woodpecker drumming on a tree trunk mingles with the singsong of winter birds in the woods.

Pinecones, the scaly brown flowers of pine trees, litter the ground until they're snatched up by the squirrels and eaten.

On rare sunny days, the bare trees become bold silhouettes and their tall trunks cast long shadows on the ground.

Look at the trunks and branches of the trees. What colors can you see? Red? Brown? Gray? Are they striped?

Peer up through the bare branches; the twiggy bundles of birds' nests are no longer camouflaged and hidden by summer leaves.

The soft, muddy ground turns hard and white with frost, and puddles freeze, cracking beneath your feet as you walk.

Springy, velvet cushions of soft green moss carpet the damp spots at the base of trees and on old wood.

As snow falls, it covers the ground and branches in a soft, thick blanket of white, insulating them against the cold.

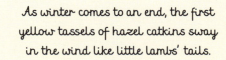

As winter comes to an end, the first yellow tassels of hazel catkins sway in the wind like little lambs' tails.

69

Into the Barn

The farmer keeps a close eye on his animals in the winter. The cows are bedded down in barns cozy with straw, and the hens, no longer laying eggs in the cold weather, roost quietly together in their coops in the yard. Out in the fields, the sheep, protected from the cold by their thick, fleecy coats, graze the grass until the snow starts to fall.

Don't forget your boots! The rainy weather and winter frost have turned the farmyard into a wet, splish-splash of mud.

Whatever the weather, the farmer is out, driving through the freezing fields to check that his flocks are safe.

Sheep, almost hidden in the white snowy fields, munch on bales of summer hay left by the farmer.

The happy moos and bellows of cows sheltering in the warm, dry barns can be heard all through the winter.

The straw and hay, collected and bailed in the summer, provide food and comfy beds for the cattle in the barns.

Chickens have lots of thick feathers to help keep them warm. They huddle together on roosts in the henhouse, waiting for the spring and for egg laying to begin.

71

Barren Lands

The countryside in winter is a barren landscape of brown earth, golden stubble, and short green growth. The hedgerows, their last leaves and berries gone, are a thicket of bare branches, cutting through the fields and shaping the view. Flocks of squawking birds follow the tractor as the farmer plows the muddy fields and feeds the dark soil while the smoke from a distant chimney drifts slowly across the land.

Fields of hay cut in the summer are now a stubbly feast of weeds and seeds for the skylarks over the winter.

As mice and shrews become tricky to find, hungry barn owls can be seen during the day hunting for food.

Behind the tractor, the farmer pulls a trailer of muck and straw from the yard. It will feed the soil to ready it for the new spring crops.

The farmer waits until late winter, when all the berries and nuts in the hedgerows are gone, and then cuts them back, neat and trim.

Climb a hill and look out at the fields below you—an endless tapestry in every shade of brown and green.

On quiet days, the farmer plows the last of the fields, shiny metal teeth turning the rich brown soil, burying the stubble below.

The first young leaves of wheat sown in the fall pop up through the cold brown earth and start to grow.

73

Frozen Waters

The pond turns to ice in winter as the temperature drops below freezing.
Fallen leaves sink to the bottom, and there is no sign of life or movement
in the still, dark water. The frozen surface turns an icy blue, and ducks,
in need of something to drink, skate across it as they come into land.
Around the edge, plants are brown and stiff with frost, and if you are
lucky, on a sunny day, a frog might stir, looking for food.

Toads bury themselves in leaves, logs,
and under the ground, safe and dry
until the temperatures start to rise.

Down in the mud at the bottom of the pond, frogs
and newts sleep through the cold winter months,
breathing through their skin.

Deep in a pile of leaves or under a stack of logs,
a grass snake coils around itself and hibernates,
waiting for the spring.

Cracks in the ice bring ducks and birds to the water, gathering around holes for an ice-cold drink.

A gray-and-white heron stands motionless on the ice before walking carefully across on its long, thin toes, wishing for a fish.

Ducks slip, slide, and skid across the frozen pond, leaving swirling silvery patterns behind them.

Beneath the ice, fish hunt out the warm pockets of water at the bottom of the pond and hide there.

Long, tall bulrushes, rigid with frost and glinting in the winter sun, line the edge of the pond.

See the ducks hurrying across the water toward you, racing to get there first as you throw bread and seeds into the pond.

Blanketed by Snow

The trees in the orchard are bare now, their leaves, fruit, and flowers long gone. Fat little buds emerge in their place, new leaves and flowers waiting for the spring. Clusters of evergreen mistletoe appear, and bright circles of lichen dot the empty brown branches. A rabbit pops up, leaving its warm burrow to search the short grass for food. Snow falls and the wind howls, but the trees stand firm, each one a black silhouette, dark against the snow.

Green mistletoe, with its pearly-white berries, hangs in bunches from the bare branches of apple trees.

Mistletoe grows when its berries are eaten by the birds. They drop the seeds, which stick to the branches and start to grow.

The orchard is left with bare trees now, naked of leaves, standing like statues in the grass.

Without leaves, the true shapes of the trees are revealed—some stand tall and straight, pointing to the sky, others are hunched and twisted, low over the ground.

Can you see the round splotches of yellow and green on the branches? These are lichen, fungi that can grow almost anywhere.

Spiky icicles of frozen water hang down from the branches. Hear them drip, drip, drip as they melt.

Rabbits forage for twigs, bark, and grass to eat now that the flowers and fruit are all gone.

Christmas trees are carried home through
the streets ready to be strung with
ornaments and colorful glowing lights.

Mind the prickly holly! Ripe red berries shine
among the spiny leaves—food for the birds and
Christmas decorations for you.

Sing along with the carol singers as the
happy songs of Christmas fill the air!

The sky turns dark early in the winter, and on clear nights, stars appear, twinkling in the black.

Sheltered in the ivy, hungry birds eat the shiny berries, still ripe when all the others have been eaten.

Did you hear the fox screaming late at night? Its shrieking howl can be a scary sound, but he is only calling for his mate.

Run and jump on the footprints in the snow—are they the same size as yours?

Twinkling Lights

Day turns to night quickly in the winter, but as Christmas approaches, the once-dark streets are full of color and light. The leaves are all gone and the gardens are bare, but cheerful wreaths decorate doors, Christmas trees twinkle at windows, and lights and decorations hang down everywhere.

A chirping robin sits by the streetlight singing through the night, and as it begins to freeze, frost patterns appear on windows, railings, and sidewalks. Be careful not to slip on the ice!

Colorful Christmas lights crisscross the street, flashing around the branches of trees and sparkling at windows.

79

Wide Eyed Editions
www.wideeyededitions.com

Written by Kay Maguire

First published in the U.S. in 2016
by Wide Eyed Editions,
an imprint of Quarto Inc.,
276 Fifth Avenue, Suite 206, New York, NY 10001

A catalog record for this book is available from the British Library.

ISBN 978-1-84780-707-6

The illustrations were created digitally
Set in Fugue, Gabriela, and Bookman Old Style

Designed by Andrew Watson
Edited by Jenny Broom

Printed in Dongguan, Guangdong, China in November 2015

1 3 5 7 9 8 6 4 2

Kay Maguire trained at the Royal Botanic Gardens, Kew in the UK, and has been writing and making films about gardening and wildlife ever since. She writes for magazines and websites and is the author of the award-winning RHS *How to Grow Your Own Crops in Pots.* She is lucky enough to live in one of London's amazing Royal Parks, where she loves growing her own food, biking, and walking the dog with her kids.

Danielle Kroll is a Brooklyn-based artist and designer. She graduated from Tyler School of Art and proceeded to work in Anthropologie's art department. Currently, she spends her days working on a variety of projects, from illustration to textiles to design. No matter what the job is, everything Danielle creates is hand-done and made with love. Her whimsical style aims to inspire curiosity and to make your day just a little bit brighter.